Copyright

eBook store:

https://www.learningarabicwithange
la.com/levantine-spoken-arabic

Facebook Group:

Join the Levantine learning Lebanese group:
"Learn Levantine Lebanese Arabic"
https://www.facebook.com/groups/680479059192
195/

Bḥib el-Maama...
I love My Mommy
بْحِب الماما

Your audio link: <u>Book Creator - بْحِب الماما</u>
<u>Bḥib el-Maama… I love My Mommy</u>

https://www.learningarabicwith
angela.com/levantine-spoken-arabic

Bḥib el-Maama…
La-anna b-ti'raale uşaş abel ma nem.

I love my mommy…
Because she reads to me stories
before I sleep.

بْحِب الماما...

لأنها بْتِقْرَالِي قُصَص قَبِل مَا نَام.

Bḥib el-Maama…
La-anna bi-t'allimne kiif a'mul
aalib gatto.
I love my mommy…
Because she teaches me how to bake a cake.

بْحِب الماما...

لأنها بِتْعَلِّمْني كِيف أَعْمُل قالِبَ غَاتُّو.

Bḥib el-Maama…
La-anna b-tekhidne maʿa 'a-s-suu'.

I love my mommy…
Because she takes me with her to the shops.

بْحِب الماما...

لأنها بْتَاخِذْني مَعها عَالسُّوق.

Bḥib el-Maama…
La-anna bi-tsarriḥle shaʻre.

I love my mommy…
Because she brushes my hair.

بْحِب الماما...

لأَنها بِتْسَرِّحْلِي شَعْرِي.

Bḥib el-Maama…
La-anna b-tekhdine
'a-l-ḥadii'a la-il'ab.

I love my mommy…
Because she takes me to the park to play.

بْحِب الماما...

لأنها بْتَاخِدْنِي عَالحَديقَة لَإلْعَب.

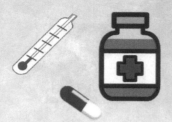

Bḥib el-Maama…
La-anna b-tiʿtine fiyye
lamma imraḍ.

I love my mommy…
Because she takes care of me
when I get sick.

بْحِب الماما...

لأنها بْتِعْتِني فِيّ لَمَّا إمْرَض.

Bḥib el-Maama…
La-anna el-maama.

I love my mommy…
Because she's my mommy.

بْحِب الماما...

لأنها الماما...

Inniheye
The End
النِّهايةِ

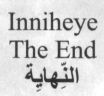

Ana bḥib…
I love…
...أنا بْحِب

Your audio link: Book Creator - I Love...
Lebanese Story

https://www.learningarabicwithang
ela.com/levantine-spoken-arabic

Ana bḥib…

I love…

أنا بْحِب...

Ana bḥib el-buuẓa!
I love ice-cream!

أنا بْحِب البُوظَة!

Mmmm

مممم

Ana bḥib "Dabduub"!

I love "Teddy-bear"!

أنا بْحِب دَبْدُوب!

ḥabiibii
حَبيبي

Ana bḥib el-maama!

I love mommy!

أَنا بْحِب الماما!

mwa!

مْوا!

Ana bḥibel-baaba!

I love daddy!

أنا بْحِب البابا!

'Abbuuta! hug!

عَبُّوطَة!

W-kamen teta w-jeddo!

And also grandma and grandpa!

وْكَمان تيتا وْجِدُّو!

Dalluu'it teta
w-jeddo!
The apple of grandma's
and grandpa's eyes!
دَلُّوعِة تِيتا وْجِدُّو!

Bas… Ma bḥib el-jazar!

But… I don't like carrots!

بَس... ما بْحِب الجَزَر!

Bas shweyy…!
Only a little!
بَسْ شْوَيّ!

Wala 'ankabuut

en-nuunuu!

And neither the itsy bitsy spider!

وَلا عَنْكَبُوت النُّونُو!

Ya Maama...!
Momy!
يا ماما!

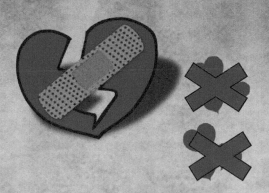

W-ma bḥib esh-shita!

And I don't like rain!

وْما بْحِب الشِّتا!

'Am tshatte!

It's raining!

عَمْ تْشَتّي!

W-yimkin…

Ma bḥibez-ziḥlayṭa el-kbiire!

And maybe…

I don't like the big slide!

وْيِمْكِن... ما بْحِب الزِّحْلَيْطَة الكُّبيرِة!

Ma badde!
I don't want to!
ما بَدّي!

Bas… Akiid bḥib
el-marjuuḥa!
But… For sure I like
the swing!
بَس... أَكيد بْحِب المَرْجوحَة!

Dawre halla'!
My turn now!
دَوْري هَلَّأ!

Inniheye
The End
النِّهايِة

Badde w-badde…
I want, I want…
...بَدِّي وْبَدِّي

Your audio link: Book Creator - I Love...
Lebanese Story

https://www.learningarabicwithang
ela.com/levantine-spoken-arabic

Marḥaba! Isme Angela.
Hello! My name is Angela.
مَرْحَبَا! إِسْمِي أَنْجِلا.

Arrab 'iid el-miiled
Christmas is near!
قَرَّب عِيد المِيلاد!

W-bade hadeya ktiir!
And I want many presents!
وبَدِّي هَدَايَا كتِير!

W-dabduub kbiir, w-byiḥke!
And a big teddy bear,
that also talks!
وْدَبْدُوب كبير، وبْيِحْكِي!

35

W-sayyaara bit-ḍaww
w bit-ṭaffe!
And a car with lights
that go on and off!
وْسَيَّارَة بِتْضَوِّي وبِتْطَفِّي!

38

...bsayne w kaleb w-arnab!
And a cat, a dog,
and a rabbit!
وْبْسَيْنِة وْكَلِب وْأَرنَبَ!

Inniheye
The End
النِّهايةِ

www.learningarabicwithangela.com

Fiyye, ma fiyyé…
I can, I cannot…
فِيِّ، ما فِيِّ...

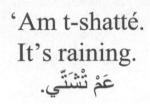

'Am t-shatté.
It's raining.
عَمْ تْشَتِّي.

Ma fiyyé ilʿab
bi-l-ṭaabé barra.
I cannot play
with the ball outside.
ما فِيِّ إِلْعَب بِالطّابِة بَرّا.

Bas fiyyé il'ab
ma' Dabduub.
But I can play
with "Dabdoub".
بَسْ فِيِّ إِلْعَبْ مَعْ دَبْدوب .

Ma fiyyé irkuḍ iddèm
el-bet maʕ aṣ-ḫaabé.
I cannot run in front of the house
with my friends.

ما فِيِّ إِرْكُضْ قِدّام البِيت مَع أَصْحابي.

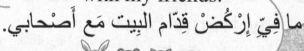

Bas fiyyé il'ab
ma' khayyé
bi-sayyaaraat es-saba'.
But I can play race cars
with my brother

بَسْ فِيِّ إِلْعَب مَعْ
خَيِّ بِسَيَّارَات السَّبَق.

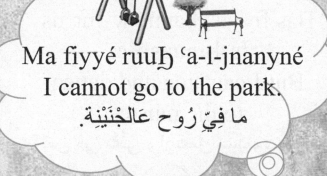

Ma fiyyé ruuḥ ʿa-l-jnanyné
I cannot go to the park.

ما فِيِّ رُوح عَالجْنَيْنِة.

Bas fiyyé ghanné w-'ur'uş
'a-l-muusii'a.
But I can sing and dance
to the music.
بَسْ فِيِّ غَنّي وْأُرقُص عَالمُوسيقَى.

Ma fiyyé ruuḩ
'a-l-dikkené w-jiib buuẓa.
I cannot go to the shop
and get ice cream.

ما فِيِّ رُوح عَالدِّكّانِة
وجِيب بُوظَة.

Bas fiyyé aʿmul aalib gatto
maʿ ikhté'.
But I can make a cake with
my sister.
بَسْ فِيِّ أَعْمُل قالِب غاتُّو
مَع إخْتي.

Ma fiyyé zuur
ḫadii'it el-ḫayawènèt.
I cannot visit the zoo.

ما فِيِّ زُور
حَديقِة الحَيَوانات.

Bas fiyyé i-'-ra
uşaş ktiir hilwé.
But I can read
Very nice stories.

بَسْ فِيِّ إقْرا قُصَص كْتير حِلْوِة.

Ma fiyyé aʿmol
Ashya mʿayyané.
I cannot do
certain things.

ما فِيّ أَعْمُل
أَشْيا مِعَيَّنة.

Bas fiyyé aʿmol
ashya ktiir ghèr.
But I can do
lots of other things.
بَسْ فِيّ أَعْمُل
أَشْيا كْتير غير.

Inniheye
The End
النِّهايِة

El-ashya el-mufaḍḍalé 'indé
My favourite things

الأشْياء المُفَضَّلة عِنْدي

Dabduubé el-mufaḍḍal
ismo Kuukuu.
My favourite teddy bear is
called Koukou.
دَبْدُوبي الُمَفَضَّل اِسْمُه كُوكُو.

Shu ism dabduub-ak/-ik
el-mufaḍḍal?
What's your favourite teddy
bear called?
شُو اِسْم دَبْدوبك الُمَفَضَّل؟

Uşté el-mufaḍḍalé hiyyé
Cinderella.
My favourite story is
Cinderella.
قُصْتِي الُمَفَضَّلِة هِيّ سِنْدِرِيلّا

Shu hiyye el-ashya
el-mufaḍḍalé 'ind-ak/-ik?
What are your favorite
things?
شو الأَشْياء المُفَضَّلة عِنْدك؟

Li'bté el-mufaḍḍalé hiyyé...
My favourite toy is...
لِعْبْتي الْمَفَضَّلِة هِيِّ......

el-'arabèyé
the stroller
العَرَبايِة

el-maṭbakh
the kitchen
المَطبَخ

uta' el-puzzle
the puzzle
(pieces)
قُطَع البازل

Akilté el-mufaḍḍalé hiyyé...
My favourite food/meal is...
أَكِلْتِي الُمَفَضَّلِة هِيِّ......

er-rez
rice
الرّزّ

el-faaşolya
beans
الفاصُولْيا

es-salaţa
salad
السَّلَطَة

Akilté el-mufaḍḍalé hiyyé...
My favourite food/meal is...
أَكِلْتِي الْمَفَضَّلِة هِيِّ.....

djèj w-riz
chicken and
rice
دْجاج وْرِز

laḥmé w-khoḍra
meat and
vegetables
لَحْمِة وْخُضْرا

samak
w-baṭaaṭa
fish and potato
سَمَك وْبَطاطا

Lawné el-mufaḍḍal huwwé...
My favourite colour is...
لَوْنِي الْمَفَضَّل هُوِّ......

el-aḥmar
red
الأَحْمَر

el-'azra'
blue
الأَزْرَق

el-'ṣfar
yellow
الأَصْفَر

Lawné el-mufaḍḍal huwwé...
My favourite colour is...
لَوْنِي الْمَفَضَّل هُوِ......

el-akhḍar
green
الأَخْضَر

el-benné
brown
البِنّي

el-
mauve
المُوف

el-banafsajé
purple
البَنَفْسَجي

Hiwèyté el-mufaḍḍalé hiyyé...
My favourite hobby is...
هِوايْتِي الُمَفَضَّلِة هِيّ.....

el-ʼrèyé
reading
القُرايِة

er-raked
running
الرَّكِض

er-rasem
drawing
الرَّسِمْ

Hiwèyté el-mufaḍḍalé hiyyé...
My favourite hobby is...
هِوايْتِي الُمَفَضَّلِة هِيِّ.....

Al'aab
el-computer
computer
games
ألْعاب الكُمْبْيوتَر

et-tiṣwiir
photography
التِّصْوير

et-tilwiin
colouring
التِّلْوين

Uuḍté el-mufaḍḍalé bi-l-bèt hiyyé...

My favourite room in the house is...

أَوْضْتِي الْمَفَضَّلِة بِالبِيت هِيِّ....

el-maṭbakh
the kitchen
المَطْبَخ

uuḍit el-'a'dé
the living room
أُوضِة القَعْدِة

uuḍit en-nom
the bedroom
أُوضِة النّوم

Uuḍté el-mufaḍḍalé bi-l-bèt hiyyé...

My favourite room in the house is...

أَوْضْتِي الْمَفَضَّلِة بِالبِيت هِيِّ......

eş-şaalon
the salon
الصّالُون

el-ḥimmèm
the bathroom
الحِمّام

el-maktab
the office
المَكْتَب

El-ḥilo el-mufaḍḍal ʿindé huwwé...
My favourite dessert is...
......الحِلُو الُمَفَضَّل عِنْدي هُوِّ

esh-shokola
Chocolate
الشُّوكولا

el-buuẓa
ice cream
البوظَة

el-gatto
cake/gateau
الغاتو

El-ḫilo el-mufaḍḍal ‘indé huwwé...
My favourite dessert is...
الحِلُو الْمَفَضَّل عِنْدي هُوِّ......

ghazl el-banèt
cotton candy
غَزْل البَنات

el-baskot
Biscuits
البَسْكوت

er-riz b-ḫaliib
rice pudding
الرِّز بْحَليب

Ryaaḍté el-mufaḍḍalé
hiyyé et-tenis.
My favourite sports
is tennis.
رِياضْتِي الُمَفَضَّلِة هِيِّ التِّنِس.

Shu hiyyé ryaaḍt-ak/-ik
el-mufaḍḍalé?
What's your favourite
sports?
شُو هِيّ رِياضْتك الُمَفَضَّلِة؟

Inniheye
The End
النّهايِة

eBook store:

https://www.learningarabicwithange
la.com/levantine-spoken-arabic

Facebook Group:

Join the Levantine learning Lebanese group:
"Learn Levantine Lebanese Arabic"
https://www.facebook.com/groups/680479059192
195/

https://www.learningarabicwithange
la.com/levantine-spoken-arabic

Made in the USA
Coppell, TX
27 April 2022